BALLPARK MYSTERIES®

#1 *The Fenway Foul-Up*

#2 *The Pinstripe Ghost*

#3 *The L.A. Dodger*

#4 *The Astro Outlaw*

#5 *The All-Star Joker*

#6 *The Wrigley Riddle*

#7 *The San Francisco Splash*

#8 *The Missing Marlin*

#9 *The Philly Fake*

#10 *The Rookie Blue Jay*

#11 *The Tiger Troubles*

#12 *The Rangers Rustlers*

#13 *The Capital Catch*

#14 *The Cardinals Caper*

#15 *The Baltimore Bandit*

#16 *The Colorado Curveball*

#17 *The Triple Play Twins*

#18 *The Atlanta Alibi*

#19 *The Black Cat Change-Up*

SUPER SPECIAL #1 *The World Series Curse*

SUPER SPECIAL #2 *Christmas in Cooperstown*

SUPER SPECIAL #3 *The Subway Series Surprise*

SUPER SPECIAL #4 *The World Series Kids*

Also by David A. Kelly

Babe Ruth and the Baseball Curse

THE MVP SERIES

#1 *The Gold Medal Mess*

#2 *The Soccer Surprise*

#3 *The Football Fumble*

#4 *The Basketball Blowout*

PICTURE BOOKS

Miracle Mud

Tee Time on the Moon

THE TWO-MINUTE WARNING

FOOTBALL MYSTERIES

by **David A. Kelly**
illustrated by **Robert Thibeault**

Curveball Books Boston

*This book is dedicated to my son Scott, who knows a flea flicker from a fumble.
Go long!*
–D.A.K.

To my family, whose love and support keep me going.
–R.D.T.

"A winner never stops trying."
–Tom Landry, head coach, Dallas Cowboys from 1960 to 1988

This is a work of fiction. Names, characters, places, and incidents either are the product of the author's imagination or are used fictitiously. Any resemblance to actual persons, living or dead, events, or locales is entirely coincidental.

Text copyright © 2023 by David A. Kelly.
Cover art and interior illustrations copyright © 2023 David A. Kelly.
All rights reserved. Published in the United States by Curveball Books, Boston.
Football Mysteries logo © 2023 by David A. Kelly.

Visit author David A. Kelly on the web at: davidakellybooks.com.
School and library author visits available at dakvisits.com.

Library of Congress Control Number: 2023912321
Library of Congress Cataloging-in-Publication Data
Names: Kelly, David A., author. | Thibeault, Robert, illustrator.
Title: The Two-Minute Warning / by David A. Kelly; illustrated by Robert Thibeault.
Description: First edition. | Boston: Curveball Books, 2023. | Series: Football Mysteries; 1 | Summary: Kate and Mike arrive in Texas to find that someone wants the Dallas Cowboys quarterback gone. Can they discover who's out to get him before they lose the big game?

Identifiers: 978-1-959378-03-7 (paperback) | 978-1-959378-04-4 (lib. bdg) | 978-1-959378-05-1 (ebook)
Subjects: | CYAC: Football—Fiction. | Dallas Cowboys (Football team)—Juvenile fiction. | Sports—Fiction. | Mystery and detective stories. | Texas—Fiction. | Cousins—Juvenile fiction. | Quarterbacks (Football)—Fiction. | Cowboys Stadium (Arlington, Tex.)—Juvenile fiction.

Printed in the United States of America.

Contents

Chapter 1	**Giddy-Up, Pardner!**	1
Chapter 2	**A Mysterious Note**	8
Chapter 3	**Telltale Marks?**	20
Chapter 4	**A Long, High Pass**	30
Chapter 5	**An Unexpected Fan**	38
Chapter 6	**A Suspect!**	49
Chapter 7	**A Giant Sign**	62
Chapter 8	**The Control Room**	76
Chapter 9	**Game Over**	85
Chapter 10	**Touchdown!**	94

End Zone Notes ☆ Dallas Cowboys   105

Giddy-Up, Pardner!

"Go wide for a bomb!" Kate Hopkins whispered to her cousin Mike Walsh.

Kate and Mike were huddled in Kate's backyard in Cooperstown, New York, on a warm fall afternoon. They loved baseball, but today was the perfect day for football. School had let out early, and they had decided to play a game against an imaginary NFL team. Orange and brown leaves fluttered across the grass.

Kate used her finger to draw an upside-down letter L on Mike's outstretched palm. It showed him the route she wanted him to run.

Mike nodded. "Got it."

The huddle broke up.

Mike leaned over a brown football opposite a pretend row of linemen. Kate stood behind him with her hands out.

"Strawberry! Blueberry! Razzleberry pie!

Hut, hut, *HIKE!*" Kate called.

Mike snapped the ball and bolted off the line.

Kate caught the snap. A trail of leaves fluttered behind Mike as he raced for the other side of the yard.

Kate cocked the ball back over her right shoulder. She launched a long, high throw deep down the right sideline. Just as she released the ball, Mike zagged to the right.

The ball arced into the crisp blue sky, spinning through the air without a wobble.

Mike glanced behind him. The football was plunging back down again. It was heading right for the very edge of the grass in front of him.

Mike poured on an extra burst of speed. He held his hands up. This was going to be close. The ball dropped straight for his outstretched fingers.

From behind the line of scrimmage, Kate cheered, "You got it! You got it! Go!"

But just as the ball touched his fingers, Mike lurched to the right. His legs twisted and his outstretched arms swung to the left as the ball just missed them. Mike crumpled to the ground while the football bounced end over end down the yard.

Kate covered her eyes with her hands. "No! No! No!" she said. "That could have been a touchdown! What happened?"

Mike lay on his back and stared up to the sky. He caught his breath and watched a couple of fluffy clouds float by.

A moment later, he popped up and smiled. He shrugged at Kate and ran over to retrieve the football.

"Sorry," Mike said as he jogged back with the football tucked against his chest. "One of those linebackers tackled me just as I touched the ball. We'll have to run that play again!"

"If this were the NFL, you wouldn't have a chance to run it again," Kate said. "That was a perfect pass!"

Mike tossed the football back to Kate. "Actually, it's only a perfect pass if the receiver catches it!" he said as he put his arm over his cousin's shoulder and smiled. "And just think, now you get another chance to work on your passing! Let's do it again."

Before they could huddle to call the next play, Kate's cell phone buzzed with a message. She pulled it out of her pocket. "Hang on," she said.

Kate read the message. A huge smile spread across her face. She pumped her fist in the air a few times.

"*TOUCHDOWN!*" she yelled.

"What?" Mike asked. "What's going on?"

"It's a message from my mom," Kate said. Kate's mom, Mrs. Hopkins, worked as a sports reporter. "And you're not going to believe it!"

"She wants to take us along to the World

Series this year?" Mike asked hopefully. Mrs. Hopkins often traveled across the country to report on baseball games. She sometimes brought Kate and Mike with her to games.

"Not this time," Kate said. "She wants to know if we could put baseball on the sidelines for the weekend."

"Why?" Mike asked.

"Because she just invited us to an NFL football game!" Kate said.

"What? Football?" Mike asked. "For real?"

Kate tossed the football straight up into the air and caught it. "Yup! For real," she said. "Giddy-up, pardner, we're going to a Dallas Cowboys game this weekend!"

A Mysterious Note

"I can't believe we get to go to dinner with Cowboys' star quarterback Carlos Cook!" Kate said as she opened the door of the rental car.

"Well, I can't believe you spent the morning doing homework!" Mike said. "I'm not doing mine until we get back to Cooperstown."

"Then I guess we'll see who does better on their report card," Kate said.

It was Saturday afternoon, and Kate and

Mike stood outside the Dallas Cowboys training facility near Dallas, Texas. They had flown in the night before with Kate's mom. She had arranged dinner with Carlos Cook, the Cowboys' star quarterback. But before that, they were going to watch the Cowboys work out.

Although professional football games take place in massive stadiums, most teams spend the week before each game getting ready in their practice facility. Practice facilities have special equipment and extra space for teams to train. They are not always near the stadium where the team plays its official games.

Kate pushed open the door to the practice facility and held it for her mother and Mike. They stopped at the security checkpoint.

"Howdy, y'all! Welcome to the Cowboys'

practice facility," the security guard said as she waved them through the checkpoint. "We've been waitin' for you! Y'all can just head down that hallway to the field. The team is already there."

"Thanks!" Mike said. As he walked through the security gate, he tossed a miniature football over the top of it and caught it on the other side.

"Looks like you should try out for the team!" the security guard said.

After the security area, Kate, Mike, and Kate's mom followed a walkway to a wide section of spongy green artificial grass on the side of the football field.

"Wow! This is as big as some college stadiums, and it's only the practice facility," Kate said, looking around. Two long stands of seats ringed the field. The end zone on the

right was colored royal blue. Overhead, a retractable roof opened on nice days.

Dallas Cowboys players in football jerseys crowded the field.

"Woo-hoo!" Mike turned and gave Kate a

fist bump. "How cool is this? We're watching the Cowboys doing a real walk-through. I can't believe we're here! Look at that—they're practicing the formations that they'll use in this Sunday's game!"

Mike took his phone out to snap a picture of the team.

"Sorry, Mike, I'm afraid you can't do that!" Kate's mother said. "No pictures allowed inside the training facility. The Cowboys can't risk someone sharing pictures of their formations or plays with the other team!"

"Oh, right." Mike blushed with embarrassment, making his freckles stand out more than usual. He slipped the phone back into his pocket.

"Hey, there's Carlos Cook!" Kate pointed to a tall, large-shouldered man about twenty feet away talking to a small group of Cowboys players. A moment later, Carlos clapped his hands and they ran out on the field. The other players took up positions.

"Ready. Set! Blue 42! Blue 42! Hut, hut!" Carlos called out.

The center snapped the football into Carlos's hands. He dropped back two steps and shifted to the right. The defensive line surged forward. A linebacker broke through and ran for Carlos. But just before the quarterback could be sacked, Carlos reared back and threw a long, spiraling pass to a player racing down the middle of the field. The ball dropped into the player's hands, and he ran the rest of the way to the end zone!

"Touchdown!" Mike yelled. "Ride 'em, Cowboys!"

As the offense regrouped for their next play, Kate's mom stepped over to the nearby stands. "I'm going to get a little work done," she said, taking her computer out of her bag.

After Mrs. Hopkins sat down, Mike and Kate played catch with Mike's small football. Then Mike noticed a full-size football on the ground. He scooped it up and tossed it to Kate. They took turns throwing it to each other on the sideline. Each time, they stepped back a few feet until soon they were lobbing long bombs to one another.

"Wow! That was awesome!" Kate said after she snagged the ball from the air.

She turned and threw it back to Mike with all her might. But instead of a nice spiral, the ball wobbled as soon as it left Kate's hand. It sailed downfield, far off target.

"Oh no!" Kate cried. The ball was drifting toward the playing field!

Mike stopped in his tracks.

He was too late!

The ball landed with a *thud* on the sideline. It bounced once onto the field.

Mike brought his hands up to his head.

The football bounced again. One the third bounce it went high into the air. And then it landed right in the middle of the Cowboys' huddle!

The huddle broke up. One of the players picked up the football. Holding it up, he stepped forward.

It was Carlos Cook!

Carlos motioned for Kate and Mike to come over. Neither of them moved. Carlos held out the football and motioned again.

Kate and Mike didn't waste another second. They dashed over.

"Howdy! Y'all must be Kate and Mike," Carlos said. He gave each of them a fist bump. "Aren't we supposed to be meeting *after* the practice?" He waggled the football. "I think this might be yours, right?"

Mike kicked at the artificial turf with his sneaker. "Um, yeah," he said. "I threw that, but it went a little wild."

Carlos smiled. "I'll say," he said. "Look, we all need to finish our practice, but I can talk with you afterward. In the meantime, try holding the football the way that I do, with my palm across the laces. Most players put their fingers on the laces, but not me."

Carlos demonstrated how he placed the laces of the ball on his palm and closed his fingers up around the side of the ball.

"Turns out there are lots of ways to hold and throw a football," Carlos said. "This one works best for me. Other players hold it all different ways. Some people say you should keep your palm off the ball and just hold it lightly with your fingertips. In any case, the secret is don't grip it too tightly. Give it a try, and I'll see y'all later!"

He tossed the ball to Mike.

As the Cowboys continued their practice,

Mike gave Carlos's method a try. He placed his palm across the laces and threw a long one to Kate.

The ball spiraled cleanly through the air and landed perfectly in Kate's outstretched hands!

"It works!" Mike yelled. "NFL, here I come!"

Kate gave him a thumbs-up and returned the throw with the same precision.

"Wow! That's great!" Mike cheered.

Mike and Kate worked on their precision throws until practice was over. As the team headed for the locker room, the two cousins walked over to meet up with Carlos.

But before they reached him, another man walked over to the quarterback from the edge of the field. He wore a silver Cowboys warm-up jacket and held a clipboard. He handed something to Carlos and left.

When Kate and Mike stepped up next to Carlos, he glanced at them.

"Oh, hi!" he said with a big smile. "I think we're set to go to dinner. Just let me read this note first." He ripped the envelope open along the top and pulled out a white note card.

On the front of the card was a crudely drawn picture of a football.

Carlos raised an eyebrow and flipped the card over to read the message on its back.

"Oh no," he said. "It's the two-minute warning!"

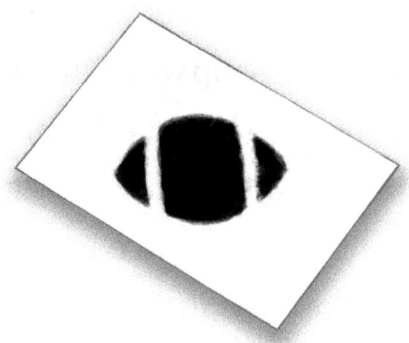

Telltale Marks?

"The what?" Kate and Mike asked at the same time.

Carlos turned the note card over and over in his hands as he shook his head. "The two-minute warning," he said. "It used to be a joke on my college team. But this doesn't look like a joke."

"What does it mean?" Mike asked.

"Have y'all read the book *Treasure Island*? It's about pirates and buried treasure.

When the pirates want to get rid of their leader, they give him a piece of paper with a black spot on it."

"But you're not a pirate, are you?" Kate asked.

"No, you're right! I'm *not* a pirate," Carlos said with a small smile. "But I *am* the quarterback for the Dallas Cowboys, and *a lot* of people want my job. See for yourself."

Carlos handed Mike the note card. He and Kate examined it. The football on the front looked like it was drawn in black marker. On the back was a message printed in big letters.

**This is your two-minute warning!
Your quarterback days are over.
Step aside or you'll be benched!**

"Whoa!" Kate said.

"I know," Carlos said. "Someone's out to get me." He looked around. Most of the Cowboys players had left practice. A group of coaches stood on the other side of the field, but no one seemed to be paying attention to Carlos.

"What about the guy who gave this to you? In the silver jacket," Kate asked. "Is it him?"

"That's Billy," Carlos said with a wave of his hand. "He's in charge of our uniforms. He told me someone in sunglasses and a cowboy hat gave him the envelope in the parking lot. He didn't think anything of it. We get lots of fan mail."

Carlos scanned the practice facility again. "I haven't told anyone else, but someone wants me gone," he said. "Look at this!" The quarterback held up his arm. He wore a big wristband with the team's plays written inside it. Carlos flipped the wristband open and reached behind the plastic window with its list of plays. He pulled out two scraps of paper and opened both of them for Kate and Mike to read.

Your team is tired of you! Retire now!
This team deserves a winner!
That means someone else, loser!

"Oh, that's bad!" Mike said.

"Someone really wants you gone!" Kate added.

Carlos slipped the notes back in his wristband. "After I started getting these notes about a week ago, I noticed some of the players seemed irritated with me," he said. "Maybe I've lost their confidence." Carlos brushed his hair back with his hand and sighed. "I don't need this before our big game against the Giants tomorrow!"

"Whoever sent you this latest note must know about it from your college days!" Mike said.

"Or maybe just someone who read *Treasure Island*," Carlos said. "An angry librarian or teacher who thinks I need to do a better job. Our fans can be pretty intense sometimes!"

"I've heard," Kate said. "How did the joke start in college?"

"Me and the guys on the football team

were all taking the same English class and reading *Treasure Island*," Carlos said. "Someone got the idea of turning the black spot into a football. We called it the fearsome football. It was supposed to send a warning, just like the black spot in *Treasure Island*. They made a card with a football on it. The message on the card said it was my two-minute warning, and I'd be hurt unless I quit. They were just teasing, but I didn't know that at first. It worried me. When they finally told me, we all laughed about it."

Carlos checked his watch. "Hey, it's getting late. I've got to stop thinking about this, because it's driving me crazy and we've got a big game tomorrow," he said. "How about we drive over to the official stadium, and I'll give you the grand tour? We can grab an early dinner after that at a steakhouse nearby."

Mike rubbed his stomach. "That sounds great. Especially the part about the steak!" he said. Mike was always hungry.

Carlos pointed to the exit at the far end of the field. "Let's go!" he said.

Kate and Mike waved Kate's mother over from the stands. They waited outside the locker room while Carlos showered and changed.

Just as they were all about to leave the practice facility, they ran into another Cowboys player in a tall white cowboy hat. He stopped directly in front of Carlos and crossed his arms.

Mike nudged Kate and glanced at the player's back. Kate tilted her head and looked.

A pair of black sunglasses dangled out of his back pocket!

"Leaving so soon, Carlos?" the man

asked. "Better be careful or maybe I'll be the one starting on Sunday!"

Carlos gave a small smile. "Kate and Mike, this is Trey Thomas," he said. "Trey's our backup quarterback."

Trey smiled wide and nodded at Kate and Mike. "Nice to meet you! But I'm not just any old backup quarterback," he said as he poked Carlos in the chest. "I'm the one they turn to when this guy gets into trouble."

Trey placed his hands on Carlos's shoulders and gave them a friendly shake. "Better be careful," he said in a deep voice. "I know we're *all* hoping you don't run into any trouble before Sunday's game!"

With that, Trey tipped his hat to Kate and Mike and stepped around Carlos. As he started walking, he let out a loud, menacing laugh!

Carlos rolled his eyes.

"What a nut!" he said. "He's a rookie, but we think he's got good potential, so we put up with him." Carlos led them through the door and pointed to a black pickup truck in the parking lot. "That's my truck. Y'all follow me to the stadium, and I'll give you a tour. After that, we'll get some dinner. See you there!"

As Mrs. Hopkins pulled the car out of the

parking lot, Kate and Mike huddled together in the back seat.

"Hey, I bet you didn't notice something funny about that backup quarterback, did you?" Kate asked.

"Sure, I did!" Mike said. "He had a cowboy hat and sunglasses, just like the person who made the threatening note."

"Nope, that's not it," Kate said.

"What was it, then?" Mike asked.

"Trey had black marks on his hands," Kate said. "The kind of marks you'd get if you were drawing a football with a black marker!"

A Long, High Pass

About a half hour later, Mike, Kate, and her mom met Carlos outside the Cowboys' stadium in Arlington, Texas.

"Zowie zoinks!" Mike said. "It looks like a giant spaceship!"

The Dallas Cowboys' massive stadium rose up in the middle of a giant empty parking lot. Its domed roof lifted at the sides to reveal huge walls of windows. Twin steel beams crossed the roof as if to keep it from rising

into space.

"It's the biggest enclosed stadium in the NFL," Kate said. "I read somewhere that you could fit the Statue of Liberty standing up inside with a few feet to spare!" Kate loved to read. On airplane rides she always read details about the cities and teams they were visiting.

Carlos led them to the main entrance. When the security guard saw him, she waved them in. They stepped into a wide-open entrance area with polished concrete floors. Carlos walked them to a row of seats overlooking the end zone and field.

"Welcome to my home," Carlos said, sweeping his outstretched arm behind him. "The Dallas Cowboys' stadium!"

The bright green football field spread out below Kate, Mike, and Mrs. Hopkins. A giant blue star outlined in silver marked the center of the field. Both end zones had thick blue stripes with COWBOYS written in large silver letters. Big yellow goalposts stood guard at either end of the field. And five huge tiers of seats stretched out in an oval all around the field.

"Wow!" Mike said. "This must be incredible on game days when all those seats are filled."

Carlos smiled. "It is!" he said. "The fans really help power us through games, so we give it our all."

Carlos pointed at the huge video display hanging over the middle of the field. "That won a Guinness World Record for the world's largest high-definition video display when it was installed," he said. "It has over ten million LED lights in it and weighs over one million pounds. That's more than eighteen fire trucks!"

Kate glanced at the field below the video display. "I'm not sure I'd want to be standing below eighteen fire trucks hanging from the ceiling," she said.

Carlos laughed. "Don't worry, it's pretty secure," he said. "I'm more worried about the defensive linemen. Some of them feel like a fire truck when they tackle you!"

The group followed Carlos along the walkway that ran around the stadium. He described exciting moment of important games as they went. They stopped at a spot overlooking the 50-yard line.

"Just remember, everything is bigger in Texas," Carlos said. "In fact, if you laid down the Empire State Building, it would fit inside this stadium!"

"If you did, a lot of people *inside* the Empire State Building would be pretty confused!" Mike said.

Carlos and Kate's mom laughed. "I guess you're right," Carlos said. "We'll skip it for now. But one thing we can't miss is the Cowboys' art collection."

"Art collection?" Kate looked around at the giant video display and goalposts on the field. "In a football stadium?"

"The Dallas Cowboys have the biggest public art collection in football," Carlos said. "It's on display around the stadium. I'll show you my favorite piece, but there is plenty of other art all over this place."

Near the escalators, Carlos pointed to a huge mural on the wall. It showed big, white exploding clouds on a deep, dark blue background.

"That's called *Blue Field Explosions*," he said. "It's by the artist Gary Simmons. I like to think it is what opposing teams see after they get hit by one of *our* linebackers!"

They rode the escalator to the lower level. "When you're here for the game, make sure to look for the mural that shows all the different words you can use to describe a win," Carlos said.

Carlos led the group around the stadium, pointing out everything from the visiting team's locker room to his favorite food stand. Finally, he guided them onto the field at the 50-yard line.

"I thought this would be a good place to end the stadium tour," he said. "Just to give you a feel for what it's like to be a Dallas Cowboys player."

Kate and Mike leaned back and looked at

the empty stadium all around them while imagining suiting up as NFL players for a big Sunday game.

Suddenly, a sharp whistle from the seating level just above them pierced the air.

Kate, Mrs. Hopkins, Mike, and Carlos all looked up. They didn't spot who made the noise. But they did see something else.

From high above, a football was plummeting straight at them!

An Unexpected Fan

"I've got it!" Mike yelled. He ran forward as the ball plunged from one of the upper decks. At the last second, he reached up and snagged the ball out of the air.

But just as he caught it, he tumbled. One foot snagged the other, and Mike went down like a Jenga tower. He

rolled over once on the field and then popped up.

"Got it!" Mike said with a big smile. He spun around and dashed back to the group. Mike skidded to a stop in front of Carlos and handed him the ball. "It's for you!"

"For me?" Carlos asked.

Mike pointed to a white note card that was taped to the ball with packing tape.

Carlos undid the tape and opened the card.

> **Everyone on the team is afraid to tell you, but we don't trust you anymore!**
> **Leave now!**

As Carlos stared at the note, Mike scanned the upper decks for a sign of who threw the ball.

Kate pointed to a railing two levels up. "It came from up there," she said. "Whoever did it is probably long gone, but let's go investigate!"

"Good idea," Carlos said. "We need to find out what's going on."

Kate, Mike, and Kate's mom ran after Carlos as he bounded back through the stadium and up the escalators and stairs. A few minutes later, they were standing at the spot Kate had pointed to.

"I don't see any sign of anyone," Mike said.

Carlos sighed and wandered to the railing. He gazed out over the field while Kate and Mike searched for clues. They checked the floor and nearby doors for anything out of the ordinary. But nothing stood out until Kate walked down the corridor.

She stopped suddenly in front of a half-opened door. She waved her arms at Mike and motioned for the group to join her. They rushed over.

Inside the open door was a white cowboy hat hanging on a hook!

"Didn't you say someone in a cowboy hat was following you?" she asked.

"I did!" Carlos said.

Kate pushed the door open the rest of the

way. They entered a big room that looked like an office. But instead of books or desks, it was filled with big pictures of the artwork in the stadium, including one of *Blue Field Explosions*.

A man stood in the corner with his back to them.

Kate stepped forward and planted her feet. "We've got you!" she said in a loud voice.

The man in the corner spun around. He opened his arms as if to welcome them.

Carlos's eyebrows spiked, and his jaw dropped.

"Carlos!" the man said. "I didn't know you were going to stop by here today!"

"Blake?" Carlos asked. He glanced at the cowboy hat and then at Blake. "Sorry, we saw the cowboy hat and thought you were someone else. Kate, Mike, and Mrs. Hopkins, this is my old college friend Blake."

Carlos looked around the room at all the art supplies. Papers, photographs, colored pencils, markers, and a couple of jars of paint were spread out on a table near the wall. "What are *you* doing here, Blake?"

"I've been here a few weeks working on an art project for the Cowboys," Blake said. "They hired me to photograph the fans looking at their artwork."

"That's cool," Carlos said. "I heard y'all had done well with your photos after college."

Blake nodded. "I have," he said. "Would you like to see what I'm working on?"

"Sure!" Kate replied.

Blake brought them over to a large table on the far side of the room. A tall woman with black hair was sitting on a stool at the table.

"This is Emma," Blake said. "She's my as-

sistant." Emma smiled as Blake introduced her.

Blake flipped through a pile of large posters on the table. Each poster showed a group of fans looking at a piece of artwork in the stadium.

"Those are great," Mike said when Blake flipped the last one over.

"Thanks!" Blake said. "I'm proud of them." He nudged Carlos. "Although, it might not be as satisfying as throwing a winning touchdown. Or being the big man on campus in college. Or marrying Susan!" Blake turned to Kate and Mike. "Back in college, everything always went Carlos's way. He was Mr. Perfect!"

"Hey, Blake, no need to be jealous!" Carlos said. "You look like you're doing well."

Blake shrugged. "I am," he said with a wave of his hand. "Things are good with me. But not as good as they are for you! Must be nice to be on TV all the time as the perfect football player!"

"Well, speaking of football," Carlos said, "how'd you like to join us for the last part of our tour? I want Kate and Mike to have a chance to throw a football on the Cowboys' field!"

Kate and Mike glanced at each other and high-fived.

"Sure," Blake said. He motioned to Emma. "Can you put all those posters away and then do what we talked about?"

"No problem." Emma slipped off her stool and started to straighten up the posters.

Back on the field, Kate's mom sat on the sidelines and checked her messages. Carlos grabbed a football and tossed it to Kate. "Here, practice that grip I showed you earlier," he said. "I'm going to catch up with Blake."

"Sure thing!" Kate called out. She and Mike ran down to the Cowboys' field to practice.

"Wow, this is amazing," Kate said as she glanced around the thousands of empty seats. "Imagine what it would be like to be playing here when this place is filled!"

"It would be incredible," Mike agreed. "As long as it wasn't filled with the Empire State Building lying on its side. Then we'd be crushed!"

Kate rolled her eyes and tossed the football from hand to hand. Then she pointed it at Mike. "Go long!" she said.

Mike took off running.

Kate stretched her arm back and let the football fly. It spiraled cleanly through the air under the giant video displays. It flew over one yard line after the other. Then it dropped into Mike's outstretched hands. Mike tucked the ball under his arm and headed straight for the end zone.

Touchdown!

"Yee-haw!" he bellowed. He spiked the ball and did a little victory dance in the end zone, just like the players did on TV. Then he turned to see if Kate had seen his dance.

She hadn't.

Instead, she was looking at someone standing near the railing on the second level up, right next to the stairs.

Someone wearing a white cowboy hat and sunglasses!

A Suspect!

Mike grabbed the ball and ran back to Kate.

"Maybe that's the guy who's after Carlos!" Mike said.

Kate glanced at the far end of the field. Carlos and Blake were standing and talking on the sideline. Her mom was still working on her computer.

"At least we know for sure it's not Blake," Kate said. "Because he's over there."

"Right," Mike said. "Maybe it's Trey. He

had enough time to follow us from the practice field. And he'd get to be quarterback if Carlos quit!"

On the second level, the figure had turned its back to the field.

"He's taking off!" Mike said. "Let's get him!"

Mike and Kate darted off the field. They zipped up the large stairs to the second level and exploded from the doorway into an empty hallway.

"Shh!" Kate held up a finger. They listened intently for the sound of footsteps. Kate turned her head sideways and glanced at the stairway door at the far end of the hallway. "I think I hear something over there. Let's go!"

Mike and Kate ran for the stairway door. A moment later, they popped through it.

The stairway landing was empty. But footsteps echoed in the stairway below them. The cousins ran over to the metal railing on the inside of the staircase and peered over the side

in time to see a man descending the stairs.

He was wearing a blue-and-white Dallas Cowboys jersey and carrying a white cowboy hat. Right before the man disappeared around the stairway corner, Mike and Kate got a good view of his face.

"Oh no!" Mike said as he turned to Kate. "Just like I thought!"

Kate nodded.

"Trey Thomas!"

* * * * *

Back on the field, Mike picked up the football he had dropped. No one had seemed to notice that they had gone on the chase.

"We need to tell Carlos we saw Trey," Kate said. "We can't prove he was the person we spotted or the one who threw the football at us, but Carlos needs to know Trey was here."

"I agree," Mike said. "But let's wait until dinner when we have Carlos alone. I don't think he'd want Blake to know what's going on."

Kate nodded. "Good idea," she said.

Mike tossed the ball to Kate. "In the meantime, we might as well get in a few more passes before we leave," he said. "I'll go long!"

Mike and Kate played catch until Carlos whistled a few minutes later. "Time for dinner!" he said as he rounded them up. "We're headed to Dusty's just a few blocks away."

"Oh, cool," Mike said. "Dusty's is great. Kate and I went there the night before a Texas Rangers baseball game."

When they stepped inside Dusty's Steakhouse a short while later, the spicy, smoky smell of mesquite barbecue hit them like a dust storm on the plains. Waitresses in cowboy hats and boots, carrying trays of sizzling steaks and ribs, rushed past the group.

"Mmm! That reminds me, I'm really hungry," Mike said as his eyes followed a platter of meat into the dining room.

"Then this is the place to be," Carlos said. "Best food in all of Texas!"

They made their way to a long wooden table with a red-and-white checked tablecloth. Above their heads hung large lights made from wagon wheels. Cattle skulls, long, pointed horns, Texas flags, and wagon parts covered the restaurant's red walls.

When a waiter in a black cowboy hat appeared, the group ordered dinner. Mike asked for the "Rancher" steak, while Kate picked Texas steak tips. Then Mike eyed the shiny metal slide next to the stairs leading to the restaurant's second floor. A group of kids had just finished playing on it. Mike nudged Kate.

"Last one down the slide is a deflated football!" Mike said.

"You're on!" Kate said. She turned to her mom. "We'll be back in a minute!"

Kate and Mike raced to the top of the stairs. They took off their sneakers and zipped down the slide.

After two times, Mike stopped Kate. "I got an idea. How about we see who can go down the slide and back up the stairs the fastest? I'll time us."

"I'll go first," Kate said. She sat down at the top of the slide.

"Go!" Mike said. Kate pushed off and flew down the slide. Mike used his phone to time her as she ran back up the stairs. "6.27 seconds!" he called out.

"My turn!" Mike said. He plopped down

on the slide but faced backward. "Watch this! Going down this way will reduce air resistance and I'll win!"

But the only thing it reduced was his time. Mike arrived at the top of the stairs in 11.23 seconds.

"Okay, okay, you won!" Mike admitted. "One last time and then we can eat!"

Kate high-fived Mike, and then they zipped down the slide and back to their table just as the food arrived.

Everyone dug into the steaks, sirloin tips, salads, giant baked potatoes, and greens that filled their plates. The group was too busy eating to talk. Finally, everything was gone.

"That was *muy rico*," Kate said as she slid back from the table. She was teaching herself Spanish and always tried to find ways to use it.

"Yes," Carlos said. "Mine was very tasty, too!" He smiled briefly but then gave a long sigh and sunk into his seat. He drummed his fingers lightly on the table.

"Everything okay?" Mike asked.

"I just don't know anymore," Carlos said with a shrug. "I forgot about things while we were chowing down, but I can't help but feel that something's bugging me!"

"The threatening notes?" Kate asked. "The feeling that your team doesn't support you?"

Carlos brushed his hand through his hair. "Yes, those will do it!" he said. "I'm worried one of my teammates is out to get me. And if the people on my team don't trust me, it's darn near impossible for me to play well. Maybe it's time to retire!"

"You can't do that!" Mike said. "Even if it *is* someone on your team, we can figure this out. Kate and I are pretty good at solving mysteries. Can we see that note again?"

"Sure." Carlos dug it out of his back pocket and handed it over. "I don't want it anymore," he said. "It'll just bring me bad luck."

Mike examined the note. The football

looked like it had been colored in with some type of black marker. Mike shot Kate a glance. Kate nodded.

"Carlos," Kate said, "there's a chance that your backup quarterback Trey Thomas has something to do with this."

"Trey?" Carlos said. "Why Trey?"

"At first, we thought it was because he seems to want your job," Kate said. "But we also noticed he had black marks on his hands when we saw him at the stadium. Just like the ones on the football note."

"Yeah, it was strange that he had black smudges on his hands," Mike added.

"It's possible, I guess," Carlos said as he rubbed his forehead. "Every player wants to be in the spotlight."

He seemed to think about it some more and laughed out loud. "Actually, I don't think it's Trey!" he said. Carlos pulled a small tube out of his pocket and yanked the cap off. He twisted the bottom of the tube, and a stick of black goo came out.

"I'll bet it was eye black on his hands, not marker from the fearsome football note," Carlos explained. He put a smudge of the stuff under his eyes. "We put this black grease under our eyes to cut down on glare from the sun or stadium lights."

Carlos laid the stick of eye black on the table and wiped off his cheek with a napkin.

"Um, actually there's something else you need to know about Trey," Kate said.

"What?" Carlos asked as he leaned forward.

"He was at the Cowboys' stadium today just after I caught the football someone threw at us!" Mike said. "When you were talking with Blake we spotted a person in a cowboy hat and sunglasses on an upper level. We ran up to investigate and saw Trey walking down the stairs!"

"Why else would he have followed you over to the stadium?" Kate asked.

Carlos looked from Kate to Mike a moment and slumped back in his chair.

"Oh," he said quietly. "Maybe it *is* Trey."

A Giant Sign

The next day, Mike, Kate, and Kate's mom arrived at the stadium two hours before the big game. It was already crowded with fans. Most were wearing blue-and-silver Cowboys jerseys, T-shirts, or hats.

Kate's mom showed Mike and Kate their seats and then went to the press box to work. Since they had time before the game, the cousins walked over to the souvenir stand. Mike spotted a Cowboys yearbook. He pulled it from the rack and leafed through it.

Kate seemed lost in thought. She twirled her long brown ponytail in circles around her finger as she stared absentmindedly at the toy footballs and Cowboys key chains for sale.

"Hmmm," she said. "If Trey really is threatening Carlos and sent that two-minute warning note, he *must* know about the fearsome football from Carlos's college days," she said. "But he's too young to have been on Carlos's college team, so how could it be him?"

"Maybe one of the *other* players on the Cowboys was on Carlos's college team," Mike said. "I've got an idea." He held up the Cowboys yearbook. "Since Blake and Carlos went to college together, maybe Blake has a copy of their college yearbook. We can compare it to this one to see if any players on Carlos's college team match players on the Cowboys today!"

"Good idea!" Kate said.

Mike bought the Cowboys yearbook at the register. Then, he and Kate headed up to Blake's office. The door was open. Inside, Blake and Emma were sorting photographs.

Mike knocked on the doorframe.

Blake looked up. "Oh, hi!" he said, waving them into the room.

"We wanted to ask you a question about Carlos," Mike said. "Something's bothering him."

Blake stopped. "That sounds serious," he said. "How can I help?"

"We think someone is out to get him," Mike said. "Someone with a cowboy hat has been sending him threatening notes."

Kate showed the note with the fearsome football to Blake.

Blake let out a whistle.

"Carlos told us someone pulled the same trick on him in college, so we wanted to ask you about it," Kate said. "Do you remember anyone suspicious on the college football team?"

"Well, I wasn't on the team," Blake said. "But I know the football players were really competitive with each other. They were jealous of the attention that Carlos got as quarterback. Heck, lots of people were jealous of him. Some of the football players probably wanted to be quarterback instead of him."

"Maybe one of them still wants to get back at Carlos," Mike said. "Do you still have a copy of the yearbook from when you and Carlos were in college?"

Blake twirled a black marker around his finger. "Oh, yeah, no problem," he said. "There's an online version. Sometimes I use it for my art projects." Blake typed a few words into a computer on the table. The screen filled with colorful pictures of college students. "This should have pictures of everyone Carlos and I went to school with."

Kate and Mike nodded. "Do you mind if we look through it?" Kate asked.

"No problem." Blake stood up and motioned for Emma to follow him. "I've got to go take pictures of the fans with the *Blue Field Explosions* mural. You can look at the yearbook as long as you want. Just leave the computer on the table and make sure to shut the door when you leave. It will lock by itself."

"Thanks!" Kate said.

Blake grabbed a black camera bag. Emma picked up a clipboard and a second camera, and they both left the office.

Kate and Mike spent the next fifteen

minutes clicking through the online yearbook. They found Carlos's and Blake's pictures, as well as lots of other students. They compared the names of the college football players to the names of the people on the Cowboys. But none matched.

"Looks like we've ruled out anyone on Carlos's college team," Mike said. "Somebody else must have sent that note."

"Right," Kate said. But she kept scrolling through the website.

The next section of the yearbook had candid photos. The captions below the pictures gave both the student's name and their nickname.

"Look at that!" Mike pointed to a picture of Carlos doing a headstand with his head balancing on a football and his toes pointing straight up. The caption said *Twinkletoes Carlos Cook on Top of His World!*

A few pages later, they came across a picture of Blake holding a big jar of pickles. Underneath it read *Picklehead Blake Barr and His Favorite Food*.

PICKLEHEAD BLAKE BARR AND HIS FAVORITE FOOD

"That reminds me," Mike said. "I'm getting hungry. I wouldn't mind some pickles right now... or maybe a hot dog with relish!"

Kate flipped through a few more screens of the college yearbook. Then she closed the computer. "You're right. We're not getting anywhere," she said. "Maybe food will help us think!"

Mike and Kate left Blake's office, making sure to close the door. On the way to their seats, they stopped at a food stand. Mike bought mac and cheese balls. Kate got a chicken-fried steak sandwich. After picking up the food, they found their seats near the 50-yard line on the Dallas Cowboys' side of the field.

The seats gave them a great view of the field and Carlos. They also had a perfect view of the giant video display above the field. Mike and Kate munched on their food as the display showed fun video clips. The crowd went wild for a series of football bloopers of players dropping the ball, jumping over other players, and running the wrong way on the field!

Mike wiped his hands on his pants when he finished. "That was yummy," he said. "Now we've just got to figure out who's sending Carlos those notes!"

"Trey is our best suspect, even if we have no idea how he knows about the fearsome football," Kate said. "He has good reason to want Carlos gone. And it doesn't look like any of the people that Carlos played with in college sent the note. Let's keep an eye on Trey during the game."

Moments later, both teams took the field and the national anthem played. When the last notes of music stopped, the crowd exploded in cheers for the Cowboys. The sound of 80,000 fans was almost deafening!

Carlos and the two other Cowboys captains jogged out to meet the referees and the New York Giants players at the 50-yard line for the coin toss. The head referee flipped the coin high into the air and let it land on the ground. She pointed to Carlos—the Cowboys had won the toss! A loud roar thundered around the stadium as the Cowboys prepared to receive the opening kickoff.

"GO, COWBOYS!" Kate and Mike yelled together.

The Giants kicker kicked the ball so far that it went through the bright yellow goalposts. That meant it was a touchback and the Cowboys would get the ball at the 25-yard line. Carlos and the Cowboys' offense jogged out to the line for the opening drive. The Giants defense lined up opposite the eleven

Cowboy players to try to stop them.

"Hut, hut, Blue 72, set, set, HIKE!" Carlos yelled.

The defensive line crashed into the offensive line. Cowboy receivers sprinted up field, darting around the defenders. Carlos heaved the ball twenty yards downfield, but a Giants defender knocked it down.

Kate and Mike watched the first quarter intently, yelling and cheering for the Cowboys, but Carlos's team couldn't find much luck on offense. As the game neared the end of the first quarter, the New York Giants had the ball. They were winning 7–0 after a long touchdown run by their star running back, Marcus Smith, earlier in the quarter.

Carlos and the rest of the offense sat on the bench in front of Kate and Mike's seats. The Giants were still some distance from the

Cowboys' end zone. The Cowboys' defensive line needed to stop the Giants from scoring or making a first down.

On fourth down, the Giants tried a short pass to their tight end, Malek Buster. But as he jumped to catch the high pass, the ball skipped off his fingertips and flew high into the air. A Cowboys cornerback dove to catch the ball before it hit the ground. The ball slipped through his hands and bounced out of bounds. Incomplete! It was now the Cowboys' ball.

Kate and Mike watched the replay on the giant video display above their heads as the Cowboys' offensive line, running backs, and receivers ran out to the field. Carlos lingered by the sideline watching the video, too.

"Hey, what's that?" Kate asked Mike. She pointed to the bottom right corner of the display where advertisements for soft drinks, food, and cars played.

But something else had popped up instead.

Mike's eyes grew wide.

It was the fearsome football!

The Control Room

"It's the two-minute warning for Carlos!" Mike said.

A giant roughly drawn football, just like the one on the note, hovered in the bottom right corner of the video display.

"That has to be like eight feet tall!" Kate said. "Somebody doesn't want Carlos to miss it!"

And he didn't!

Carlos was staring up at the fearsome football.

The image lingered for a moment longer. Then it disappeared, replaced by an ad for fruity red PowerPunch.

Nobody else seemed to have paid attention to the fearsome football besides Kate, Mike, and Carlos.

Carlos glanced around as if searching for someone. He seemed nervous. Even though the rest of his team had already taken the field, Carlos didn't move from the sideline.

A coach with a bulky black headset jogged over to Carlos. He patted the quarterback on the back. Shielding his mouth with a clipboard, the coach said something to Carlos. Carlos nodded. He pulled his helmet on and rushed out to the field.

The Cowboys huddled and then broke for the play.

Carlos lined up five yards behind the center.

"Red 64, blacktop, ranger, set, set, HIKE." The Cowboys' center snapped the ball toward Carlos's chest. As Carlos backpedaled, the ball slipped out of his fingers and bounced on the turf. Carlos dove on the ball. Instantly a pile of Giants defenders covered him up. The crowd groaned as the referees marked the ball down.

It was now second down, and the Cowboys had even farther to go to make a first down.

The next two plays weren't much better. Carlos tried a disastrous long throw that went wildly off the mark. On third down, he passed again. It was intercepted! The New York Giants ran the whole way down the field to score.

The Giants led 14–0!

Fans nearby booed and jeered.

"Come on, Cowboys!" one fan screamed. "We need to score!"

Kate shook her head. "This doesn't look good," she said. "Carlos seems spooked!"

"It's the two-minute warning!" Mike groaned. "He saw it on the video screen, and it's throwing him off. Someone put it up there to get in his head."

Kate stared at the giant video display. "Yes, someone did put it up there," she said. "And I know how to find out who!"

Kate bounded up the aisle as Mike followed. She stopped to ask a security guard something. The guard pointed to the nearby stairs.

After more flights of stairs than they could count, Kate and Mike reached the upper level of the stadium.

"Where are we going?" Mike asked when

they finally slowed down.

Kate didn't answer right away. Instead, she stopped in front of a large metal door. It was open.

"Here," she said.

A sign next to the door read VIDEO CONTROL ROOM. Inside the medium-sized room, a handful of women and men sat behind banks of computer screens. Huge windows overlooked a corner of the field below.

"These people manage all the video feeds that get displayed on the giant screen," Kate said.

A dark-haired woman in front of the nearest computer looked up. "Can I help y'all?" she asked. "You're not lost, are you?"

Kate stepped forward. "No, ma'am, we're not lost," she said. "And yes, thanks, we'd like some help. My name is Kate, and this is my cousin Mike. We're trying to solve a mystery for Carlos Cook. We have a question about something that was just shown on the video display."

"Well, shoot!" the woman said. "I'm happy to help anyone who wants to help Carlos."

"Sorry to bother you in the middle of the game, but it's important." Kate handed the

mysterious note to the woman. "Carlos got this yesterday. A picture of that same football just appeared on the main display screen a little while ago."

"And when it did, it spooked Carlos. He messed up some plays," Mike said. "Is there some way you can check who wanted that picture displayed?"

The woman looked down on the field. The Cowboys were still losing. Carlos had just fumbled the ball. She nodded. "I don't know if it will help y'all," she said. "But I'll see who purchased the ad."

She hit some buttons on the keyboard and searched her computer display. "Someone named P. Head bought it a few days ago," she said.

"That's it?" Kate asked. "No address or phone number?"

The woman shook her head. "Not in our system," she said. "Try the business office on Monday morning. I'm sure they can look it up for you. I'm sorry there's not more I can tell you now."

She handed the note back to Kate. "Thanks," Kate said. "You've been very helpful."

Kate and Mike left the video control room.

"P. Head? That's useless. We can't wait until Monday!" Mike said. "We need to find out who's after Carlos *today*, before the end of the game!"

They started to walk down the empty hallway, but after a few steps, Kate stopped. Her eyebrows pulled together. "P. Head, P. Head. P. Head," she said. "That sounds familiar."

"Parker Head? Preston Head?" Mike said. "Lots of names start with P."

Kate continued to repeat the name. Mike was just about to give her a shove when she snapped her fingers.

"I've got it!" she said. "I know who sent the fearsome football!"

Mike jumped in front of Kate. "You do?" he asked. "Who?"

"Blake!"

Game Over

"What?" Mike asked. "Blake?"

"Picklehead!" Kate said. "P. Head is Picklehead! And Picklehead was Blake's college nickname! We saw it in their college yearbook on Blake's computer!"

"That means that Blake sent Carlos the fearsome football!" Mike said. "But why?"

"Because he's jealous of Carlos," Kate said. "Remember what he said about Carlos being on TV all the time?"

Mike nodded.

"Think about it." Kate ticked off the reasons on her fingers. "One, his nickname matches up with the person who bought the ad. Two, he was in college with Carlos, so he knew about the fearsome football. Three, we saw black markers and a cowboy hat in his office. And four, he's been here at the Cowboys' stadium for a while working on his art project, so he could have sent the multiple notes."

"Yeah," Mike said. "And he's got the motive! He's jealous that Carlos is famous! You could be right. But can we *prove* it?"

Kate looked down at the field and nodded. Only one minute remained before halftime. "We don't need to prove it if he admits it!" she said.

Mike rolled his eyes. "I don't think Blake is just going to admit it," he said.

"Maybe he will," Kate said. "I've got an idea." She took the note and a pen out of her pants pocket and wrote something on the back of it. Then she slipped it back into her pocket. "Now, all we need to do is find Blake."

"He said he was going to be photographing the *Blue Field Explosions* mural today," Mike said. "Let's start there!"

They ran through the giant hallways of the Cowboys' stadium until they reached a series of escalators. "I think we need to go down a level or two," Mike said as they hopped on.

Kate scanned the stadium for the artwork as they rode down. "There's the mural!" A large blue mural decorated a wide wall above and beside the escalator. The escalator reached a landing. But Blake wasn't there. Mike and Kate raced to the next escalator segment and headed down to the next level.

"There he is!" Mike said. Blake and Emma were standing off to the side at the bottom of the escalator with a large camera. Blake was taking pictures of fans with *Blue Field Explosions* in the background above them.

Mike and Kate bounded off at the bottom of the escalator and ran up behind Blake. He was finishing up a picture of a boy and a girl wearing blue-and-silver Cowboys jerseys. When the kids stepped away, Kate tapped Blake on the shoulder.

Blake spun around.

"Oh, hi!" he said. "What is it?"

"Blake, we have a question for you," Kate

said. She pulled out Carlos's threatening note and handed it to him.

Blake squinted at the card. "You already showed this to me yesterday."

"I know," Kate said. "But there's something on the back we wanted you to see."

Blake flipped it over. He stared at the bottom of the card. His shoulders sank when he read what Kate had written on the back.

> **This Two-Minute Warning note card was brought to you by Picklehead Blake Barr!**

Blake flipped the card over and straightened up. He handed the note back to Kate. "What kind of joke is this?" he asked. "I don't get it."

"I *think* you do," Kate said. "We talked with the people running the video display. They said the football ad was bought by someone named P. Head. And P. Head stands for Picklehead, your nickname in college!"

Blake's eyes widened. "What? How did you know my college nickname was Picklehead?" he asked.

"It was in the yearbook," Mike said. "It all connects. You're jealous of Carlos's fame, and you've been sending notes because you're here at the stadium."

"You wanted to teach him a lesson, didn't you?" Kate asked.

"You wanted him off the team, didn't you?" Mike added.

Kate waved the note in the air. "Stadium security is going to be very interested in the facts behind this note," she said.

Blake's eyes narrowed as he looked from Mike to Kate to the note. He tried to look menacing. But he wasn't. Suddenly, his shoulders slumped, and he let out a sigh.

"Oh, you're right," Blake said with a shrug. "I did it. I'm tired of him *always* getting everything. He *always* wins. He got the NFL contract and the spotlight! It's not fair! It wasn't fair in college, and it's still not fair!"

"So, you tried to threaten him by following him around in a cowboy hat and sunglasses to scare him?"

Blake nodded. "I wanted to make *him* feel unlucky for a change."

Kate pointed to Blake's assistant, Emma. "I'll bet she's in on it, too," Kate said. "You must have had her dress up in the cowboy hat, sunglasses, and Cowboys jersey when you came down on the field with Carlos, just to give yourself an alibi!" she said.

"Yeah, that was Emma," Blake muttered quietly while staring at the floor.

"Then Trey isn't involved?" Mike asked.

Blake didn't move for a moment. Then he shook his head no.

"You were just trying to make him look like a suspect," Mike said. "What did you do, send him a message to follow us to the stadium so it would look like he threw the football with the threatening note, even though you or Emma actually threw it?"

"Every backup quarterback wants to be quarterback!" Blake said with a shrug. "I simply sent him a note telling him to come to the upper level of the stadium for some inside info on how to become the new Cowboys quarterback."

"But there wasn't any info there?" Mike asked.

Blake groaned, shook his head, and stared at Mike and Kate. "You're quite the little detectives, aren't you?" he said.

"Well, we *are* good at observing some things," Kate said.

"And figuring other things out," Mike said. "Like how you were jealous of Carlos."

"Of course, I'm jealous!" Blake snorted. "I wanted to throw *him* off *his* game for once!"

Mike leaned in near Blake.

"Well, now the game's over for *you*," he said.

Touchdown!

Down on the field, the game wasn't over for Carlos yet. But it felt like it.

The Cowboys were behind by 14 points at halftime, and the mood around the stadium was glum. Fans were unusually quiet while standing in line at the food stands or walking the hallways. Carlos and the Cowboys had to get better fast if they wanted a chance at winning the game.

Kate and Mike raced through the stadium to find Carlos before it was too late. But first they had stopped to alert stadium security to Blake's plan.

"Halftime's almost over!" Kate called out to Mike. "Where's Carlos?"

Mike pointed to a section of seats below them. The entrance to the Cowboys' locker room was below the seats. "He'll come out of that tunnel," he said.

Kate and Mike ran down the aisle right above the entrance from the Cowboys' locker room. They took the steps two at a time until they reached a railing by the field.

Moments later, the Cowboys' mascot, a cowboy with a huge head, ran out of the tunnel. He was followed by an almost never-ending line of the Dallas Cowboys cheerleaders, dressed in white cowboy boots, white shorts, blue shirts, and white vests. They waved silver, white, and blue pom-poms as they danced onto the field.

Mike nudged Kate. "Watch for Carlos!" he said. "We need to get his attention as soon as he gets on the field or he won't hear us!"

The crowd exploded in cheers when the Cowboys hit the field a minute later. The players ran out, pumping their arms and jumping. They looked excited for the second half!

At least most of them did. Carlos straggled behind the others. His shoulders were down, and he was walking instead of running. It wasn't a good sign.

"There's Carlos!" Kate yelled.

"Carlos! Carlos! Carlos!" Mike and Kate yelled together, as loud as they could.

Carlos slowed for a second and started to turn around.

But then he shook his head and sped up,

running onto the field!

"Oh, no!" Kate said as nearby fans started to sit down in their seats. "We missed him!"

Mike leaned against the railing and started to call out, but Carlos was too far away. They had lost their chance!

Kate started walking up the aisle. After about five steps, she felt a tug on the back of her shirt.

"Look at that!" Mike said. "Carlos is on the

bench with his helmet off. If we move over a section, maybe we can get his attention!"

They ran over to the next seating section and bounded down the aisle to the railing. Carlos was rolling his head from side to side, stretching his neck.

Mike leaned as far over as he could and put two fingers between his lips.

Phwwwwwhht!

His whistle split the air.

"Carlos!" Kate yelled.

For a moment, nothing happened. Then Carlos turned around. Kate and Mike waved and called his name.

Phwwwwwhht!

Mike whistled again.

Carlos spotted them!

He stood up and said something to a nearby coach. Then he jogged over to them.

On either side of Kate and Mike, fans went wild with cheers.

"What's up, y'all?" Carlos asked. "What's so urgent?"

"We found out who sent the two-minute warning!" Kate said.

"And who was following you!" Mike added.

Carlos's eyes widened. "You did?" he said. "That's great!" He reached up and gave Kate and Mike fist bumps. "Who?"

"Blake!" Kate said. "He's jealous of all your success!"

Kate and Mike quickly explained how they had solved the mystery of the football threat and the mysterious stalker. When they were done, a big smile spread across Carlos's face.

"This means it's not Trey or one of my teammates!" Carlos said. "They still have faith in me!" He gave Kate and Mike a thumbs-up. "Thanks! This makes all the difference."

Carlos ran back to the bench. He picked up his helmet and dashed onto the field.

Kate and Mike looked at each other. "We did it!" Mike said.

"Woo-hoo!" Kate cheered.

The cousins high-fived.

They were back in their seats before the second half started.

When the Cowboys took the field, it was clear that Carlos was his old confident self again.

On the first play of the next drive, he threw a monster long bomb to his speediest receiver, Antoine Jones. Jones sprinted past the entire Giants defense for an 80-yard touchdown!

After the Cowboys kicked the extra point,

the Giant's lead was cut in half!

Five minutes later, the Cowboys scored their second touchdown in a row and another extra point to tie the game. Over the next twenty minutes, the Cowboys scored three more touchdowns to the Giants' one!

By the end of the game, the Cowboys were up by 14.

Carlos was electric in the second half. He completed passes to all his open receivers and eluded the Giants' aggressive linebackers as they blitzed through the line to try to sack him.

As the clock ran out, the coaches and players swarmed the field to congratulate Carlos. Confetti cannons shot out paper streamers.

"That was great!" Kate said.

Kate and Mike sat back and watched the celebration. As the field started to clear, they looked for Carlos. But they couldn't find him amid the reporters, coaches, and players moving around on the field.

Finally, about fifteen minutes later, Kate pointed to the right. "There he is!"

Carlos was standing next to the far side of the Cowboys' sideline bench. He was motioning them to join him.

Kate and Mike walked down the aisle. Carlos opened the gate onto the field.

"Thanks so much for figuring out that Blake did it," Carlos said to them. "Security has been interviewing him. He confessed the whole plan. Y'all were right—he sent me all those warning notes. He was getting back at me for winning all the time."

"I guess he really wanted to mess up your season," Mike said.

"He sure did!" Carlos said. "But y'all know

what they say in Texas. Letting the cat out of the bag is a whole lot easier than putting it back in. And now that Blake's plan is out of the bag, he's going to be facing some serious trouble. Alice, our chief of security, will decide what happens to him next."

"And you can get back to football," Mike said, "without worrying about your job."

"Or your teammates!" Kate said.

Carlos nodded, and his face relaxed into a big smile. "I'll tell you what," he said. "Y'all are pretty good detectives. Now that my head is on straight, we're fixing to make it to the Super Bowl this year. And if we do, how'd y'all like to come as my special guests?"

"Yee-haw!" Mike whooped.

Kate pretended to spike a football. Then she did a little happy dance. "Yes, sir!" she said. "We'd love that!"

Carlos gave Kate and Mike high fives.

"Then it's a plan!" he said. "Let's go celebrate Texas-style with some barbecue, chili, and sweet tea!"

FOOTBALL MYSTERIES

End Zone Notes

A Slow Start But Strong Finish. The Dallas Cowboys were founded as an expansion team in 1960. Until that time, there hadn't been an NFL team south of Washington, DC. Tom Landry was their first coach and remained their coach for twenty-nine seasons. Initially the team lost a lot, but within five years it became a much better team. As of 2023 it has gone on to win five Super Bowls and eight NFC conference championships. Jerry Jones purchased the team in 1989 and became its owner, president, and general manager. Over the years, he's had an oversized impact.

Ice Bowl. The 35th NFL Championship Game featuring the Dallas Cowboys and the Green Bay Packers became known as the Ice Bowl. It was played on December 31, 1967, at Lambeau Field in Green Bay, Wisconsin. It determined which team would proceed to the Super Bowl. The game time temperature was −15 degrees, with a windchill of around −48 degrees. In other words, it was COLDER than COLD! In fact, it was so cold that when the referee blew the whistle to start the game, it froze to his lips! It's ranked as one of the best games in NFL history. Unfortunately for the Cowboys, they lost 21–17.

Lone Star logo. The logo for the Dallas Cowboys is a blue star. It represents the Lone Star State, a nickname for Texas.

America's Team. The Dallas Cowboys are known as "America's Team." They were given that nickname in a 1970s season highlight film, and it stuck. The Dallas Cowboys consistently rank as the NFL's most valuable team (worth $8 billion in 2023). They also have the most fans attending their games (over 800,000 in 2022), and they are the most searched football team on the internet!

Home on the Range. The Cowboys have moved around a bit. They started out playing in the Cotton Bowl, a stadium that opened in 1932. They played there from 1960 (when the team was founded) until 1971. After that, the Cowboys moved to Texas Stadium, a domed football field just outside the city of Dallas. They played there from 1971 until 2008. Then they moved to Cowboys Stadium (now called AT&T Stadium) in Arlington, Texas, in 2009. That's the stadium featured in this book. It seats 80,000 fans but can be expanded to fit 100,000 and is one of the biggest domed stadiums in the world.

Rivalries. The Cowboys have deep rivalries with a variety of teams, including the Washington Commanders, the Philadelphia Eagles, and the New York

Giants. When it comes to Super Bowls, the Cowboys and Pittsburgh Steelers have played more matchups than any other teams in the National Football League (NFL).

How About Them Cowboys? After Cowboys coach Jimmy Johnson called out "How 'bout them Cowboys?" in the locker room after the team's exciting win against the San Francisco 49ers in January 1993, the phrase stuck. The Cowboys went on to win the Super Bowl three out of the next four seasons. Fans love to use the phrase to express their love of the team.

Famous Players. Over the years, the Dallas Cowboys have had lots of famous players on the team, including Tony Romo, Herschel Walker, Emmitt Smith, Troy Aikman, Bob Lilly, Drew Pearson, Ed "Too Tall" Jones, Lee Roy Jordan, and Roger Staubach.

A Handful of Super Bowls. The Cowboys have won five Super Bowls. That's enough for a Super Bowl ring on every finger of one hand!

Read more from David A. Kelly

★ About the Author ★

DAVID A. KELLY played plenty of backyard football when he was young, but he never made it to the NFL. So now he's writing about it in the *Football Mysteries* series. David is best known for his *Ballpark Mysteries* and *Most Valuable Players* series of sports mysteries books, and his picture books *Miracle Mud* and *Tee Time on the Moon*. He lives in Newton, Massachusetts, with his family.

Visit davidakellybooks.com for more information.
Visit dakvisits.com for information on school visits.